49
Things to do on the Big Island

The opinions are those of the author, his wife, and their cats; the dogs are happy all the time and have no opinion. Any resemblance to persons living or dead is coincidental, except for actual people identified by name. While this is a true and accurate depiction to the best of my knowledge, the author assumes no liability for damages resulting from this book. Don't blame me if you are allergic to pineapple or can't swim or something.

Also by Sam Cudney

Declare His Praise in the Islands – The history of Christianity in Hawai'i

Illustrated Tour of Sacred Places in Hawai'i – Tour guide to locations with special significance to Hawaiians

Welcome to Paradise: Moving to Hawai'i Made Easy (sort-of) – A guide to the ins and outs of moving to Hawai'i

Hawai'i A Glimpse into the Past – Illustrated history of Hawai'i in the context of world events

How to Publish Your Book for Free – A real-world how-to guide to independent publishing.

Cheap Fun in Hawai'i – Have a knockout vacation without going broke. Getting here, things to do.

all available through Amazon at -

http://tinyurl.com/books-by-sam

Copyright 2014, 2015, 2016 Sam Cudney

All rights reserved

Contents

Introduction, and Welcome	1
How to use this Book	3
Coffee Country Tour	7
Mamalahoa Highway	*12*
Hula Daddy	*12*
Coffee Plantations	*13*
Holualoa	*14*
Kuakini	*14*
Daifukuji Soto Mission	*15*
Amy B. H. Greenwell Ethnobotanical Garden	*15*
Greenwell Farms	*16*
Kealakekua Bay	*16*
Captain Cook	*16*
Puʻuhonua o Hōnaunau National Historic Park	*18*
St. Benedictʾs Catholic Church	*19*
Uchida Farm	*20*
Northern Island Tour	23
Puʾukohola National Historic Site	*26*
Spencer Beach Park	*27*
Kawaihae	*28*

49 Things to do on the Big Island

Hamakua Macadamia Nut Factory	*29*
Hawi	*30*
Saint Augustine Episcopal Church	*32*
Kapa'au	*33*
Kalahikiola Congregational Church	*35*
Pololu Valley	*35*
Kohala	*36*
Waimea	*36*
Northeast Tour - The Hamakua Coast	**39**
Saddle Road	*41*
Cinder Cone	*42*
Mauna Kea Visitor's Center	*43*
Mauna Loa	*44*
Hilo	*45*
Akaka Falls	*48*
Kalopa State Recreation Area	*48*
Honoka'a	*48*
Waipio Valley	*49*
Waimea	*50*

49 Things to do on the Big Island

See a Volcano - Southern Tour   53
Ho'okena Beach Park   *54*
Southpoint   *55*
Punalu'u Beach Park   *55*
Hawai'i Volcanoes National Park   *56*
Ahalanui Park   *58*
Hilo   *58*

Kailua-Kona History Tour   61
Mokuaikaua Church   *62*
Hulihe'e Palace   *63*
First Catholic Mass   *63*
Ironman Triathlon   *65*

Other Fun Things   67
Have a Picnic   *67*
See Hula   *71*
See Manta Rays   *72*
Take a Hike   *73*
Bird Watching   *73*
Check out Some Petroglyphs   *75*
Have Breakfast at a Farmers' Market   *77*

Afterword   79

＃ 49 Things to do on the Big Island

Introduction, and Welcome

Introduction, and Welcome

Welcome to Hawai'i! I hope you have a wonderful stay, and plan on coming back.

Naturally, you'll spend lots of time at the beach, and there are some great guides to the beaches. But there is much more to do in Hawai'i than go to the beach. When you get waterlogged and sunburned, or just plain worn out, you'll look for other things to do. No problem!

You will find display racks of cards and activity booths just about everywhere, enticing you with offers of snorkel trips, dinner cruises, ziplines, helicopter rides, luaus, wilderness tours, whale watching tours, swimming with dolphins, paranormal tours, and just about every other imaginable activity.

49 Things to do on the Big Island

But there are also tons of things that are free or really inexpensive. You won't find display cards for most of them because they're free, or not well known. That's where this book comes in.

Here are a bunch of free or very inexpensive things you can do on Hawai'i Island, including several self-guided tours that will introduce you to the rich history and culture of Hawai'i. The most expensive costs about $15, and most are free. All you need is transportation. Conspicuously absent is "watch a sunset;" you have probably already figured that one out.

One more thing; if you have an idea for something that you think should be included, let me know!

Now go have fun.

How to use this Book

How to use this Book

I've arranged most of the things in this book into five self-guided tour routes, each with half a dozen or more attractions. It's unlikely that you would want to see, or could see, all of the things along each route. The idea is that you identify those things you want to see or do and string them together along the route as your own personal, customized tour.

Each tour route is organized as a general overview and driving directions, followed by additional information about **highlighted (like this)** points of interest.

The longest trip, the southern route to Hawaiian Volcanoes National Park, is a day excursion of about 200 miles from West Hawai'i and back, taking 4 to 5 hours of driving time, past black and green sand beaches, a hot spring you can swim in, rain forests, and the southern-most point in the United States.

The shortest is a walking tour of the historic north part of Kailua-Kona. It takes about an hour in which you visit an ancient temple, the first church in Hawai'i, and a royal residence. The others are easy day trips. Read through the points of interest for each tour route for more details.

I've also included a few things that don't fit with the tour routes and that are worth looking into. I suggest you flip through the book and briefly skim the headings to see what interests you, then plan your trips accordingly.

This book is deliberately short. You can find lots more details about each location or activity, but in the interest of

3

49 Things to do on the Big Island

brevity I have covered only the highlights. You will notice that the big island is pretty rural; presumably, that's part of its appeal to you. The activities I suggest are also pretty rural in nature; places to go, things to see.

Driving on the big island can be frustrating if you're in a hurry. The highest speed limit is 55, and that only in a few places. Roads are mostly 2-lane, twisty, and slow; it appears that they were made by laying asphalt over goat trails. Traveling 2 or 3 miles can take 20 minutes, which can be annoying until you get used to it; it seems like it should be quicker, but it isn't. You will also notice that road designations change seemingly at random; Highway 19 turns into Highway 11, then back to 19 again, etc. It just is that way.

When you haven't packed a picnic, stop to eat at one of the local places instead of a chain. Fast food is the same everywhere, except it's more expensive here. Also, there can be an inverse correlation between the quality of the view and the quality of the food at the fancier places. There are exceptions, of course, but if the restaurant is pushing their view and drinks, the food may not be worth mentioning.

Pick up a road map (if you fly Hawaiian Airlines, they'll offer you one before you land) but don't assume it's the final word. There can be inconsistencies between maps and reality, so you might have to hunt around a bit in some areas. GPS's can sometimes be misleading, too; or the GPS might not accept an address. Big island street addresses are two digits, a space or hyphen, and three to five more digits.

Let's go!

How to use this Book

49 Things to do on the Big Island

Coffee Country Tour

Coffee Country Tour

Tour a coffee plantation, see amazing historic sites, visit a top-notch snorkeling spot, swim with dolphins if you're lucky. This can take anything from a few hours to all day, depending on how often you stop, for how long, and how far you want to go. The distances do not sound like much; two miles here, three miles there, but they can be slow miles.

The Kona district of Hawai'i is world famous for its coffee. Even if you're not a coffee drinker, the journey from tree to cup is interesting in itself. If you are a coffee drinker, you've hit the mother lode.

The Kona coffee belt is the region extending from Kailua-Kona to the south, at an elevation of 1500-2500 feet. In other words, it's along the **Mamalahoa** Highway, or Hawai'i Belt Road. This is the upper road, State Road 190, not the coast road. You get there from the resort areas along the Kohala Coast by going up the Waikoloa Road to the Mamalahoa Highway; and from the Kona area by going up either Hina Lani (the road that serves Costco and Home Depot), Palani Drive, or Henry Street (the road that serves Walmart, etc). Henry Street joins Palani Drive just above Walmart. Both routes are a steep climb.

If you're coming from Hilo, take the Saddle Road to the Mamalahoa Highway and turn south.

If you take the Waikoloa Road, turn right and go south along the highway about 25 miles or so through some ever-changing scenery. You'll see what they mean about the many different climate zones on the Big Island. There are

49 Things to do on the Big Island

several places to stop and see the sights. Some of the visible lava flows are fairly recent, from the early 19th century.

As travel south approaching Kona you will see Hina Lani Street on your right; almost immediately after, the road forks at a "T" intersection, with the straight leg heading down the hill to the right. That's Palani Road, to Kona. The fork to the left, marked to Holualoa, goes around a pretty sharp curve and disappears in the trees. That's the road you want; take the left fork.

If you came up Hina Lani, turn right onto the Mamalahoa Highway, followed almost immediately by a left at the fork. If you came up Palani from Kona, make a sharp right turn onto the fork.

You're now at the very north end of the coffee belt. All through the coffee belt you'll see signs offering tours and tastings. Most of the small growers are personable and have good coffee; every farm is a little different. Unless you're absolutely crazy about coffee, or writing a book about coffee farming, pick one or two and skip the rest. Otherwise, you'll be so caffeinated you won't need a car, you'll just run the rest of the way.

Conveniently, one of the better coffee tours appears almost right away. The road winds like a snake (of which there are none in Hawai'i) for a half mile from the intersection with Palani Road to **Hula Daddy Coffee.** It's the small-ish green building with a clock tower to the right, below the road. That's it. Stop there and refresh yourselves.

After you've sampled to your heart's content, you can either stop now and go back to Kona, or continue on along

Coffee Country Tour

the road and plan on spending a while touring the coffee country and points south. There're lots more **coffee plantations** offering tours.

After four slow miles you'll come to the little artsy town of **Holulaloa**, another old mountain town, with the usual assortment of galleries and historical buildings. From there you can continue on down through the coffee belt.

By this time you'll have noticed that flat land is nonexistent along the road, and that it has more twists than a knotted rope. Give up all thoughts of high speeds and fast roads. Enjoy the scenery.

Another two slow miles takes you to a fork in the road at about mile marker 114. The right fork goes down the hill to join the **Kuakini** Highway, while the left is more of the "Mamalahoa Kona Heritage Corridor", the road you want. It's a narrow, winding road through a dense forest.

After yet another slow two miles, on the mauka (inland) side in Honalo at about mile marker 111 or so you'll a red Buddhist temple, the **Daifukuji Soto Mission**. You're welcome to stop in. This is a "Y" intersection; the downhill leg to your right and back joins the coast road below. Continue straight ahead through Honalo. At mile marker 110, is the **Amy B. H. Greenwell Ethnobotanical Garden**.

You next pass through the little towns Kainaliu, with the historic Aloha Theatre and the 1867 Lanakila Church, and Kealakekua, and eventually come to the town of Captain Cook, two miles south of the Buddhist temple and "Y" intersection in Honalo.

49 Things to do on the Big Island

Between the towns of Kealakekua and Captain Cook you'll find **Greenwell Farms**, a major coffee grower and packer.

Continuing south on the highway, now a bit straighter and faster, you have a choice of routes, depending on what you want to do;

- You can turn down Napo'opo'o Road (160) just south of the town of Captain Cook, at roughly mile marker 110. The intersection is 1.5 miles from the stoplight at the McDonalds, and easy to miss. If you miss the turn, you can continue on to the second option, below. Otherwise, go downhill to **Kealakekua Bay** and the **Captain Cook** Monument, passing Painted Church Road on the way. Admire the view, then go then south 3 miles on the road to **Pu'uhonua o Honaunau** National Historical Park and the "two step" snorkeling spot, then left and uphill at **Painted Church** Road to the Mamalahoa Highway. This takes you through the 1792 battlefield of Moku'ōhai, one of Kamehameha's first victories.

- Alternatively, you can continue on to mile marker 104, where you make a hard right turn onto road 160. You can either turn right on **Painted Church** Road, then continue back up to a right turn on Middle Ke'ei Road, then up to the Mamalahoa Highway, or continue a short distance to **Pu'uhonua o Honaunau**. From the National Park you can either backtrack to Painted Church road and up the hill, or continue to **Kealakekua Bay,** then up Napo'opo'o Road to the Mamalahoa Highway. This route is a bit more complicated.

Coffee Country Tour

By now, the formerly slow Mamalahoa Highway seems like a superhighway. As you head north, located between Middle Ke'ei Road and Napo'opo'o Road at about mile marker 107, is, yes, another coffee tour; the Royal Kona Visitor Center, with a self-guided tour and museum, and of course, free samples. Slightly north of that is **Uchida Coffee Farm**, an early 20th century coffee farm preserved and operated as it was 100 years ago.

This area is a maze of small roads leading to interesting things, and it's impossible to get really lost. Delayed, yes; but not really lost. Most roads end at the ocean on one end, and the Mamalahoa Highway at the other. Many of the roads in the area are one-lane with ferocious speed bumps, so beware.

Head back north on the Mamalahoa Highway as far as you like, getting a second chance at anything you missed; the side road at the stoplight in Captain Cook, next to the McDonald's, drops steeply down to an extension of the coast road that eventually turns into Ali'i Drive. The Kuakini Highway branches off of the Mamalahoa Highway at Honalo, right next to the Buddhist temple. Either way takes you back north to Kona.

49 Things to do on the Big Island

Coffee Country Tour Points of Interest
Mamalahoa Highway
The road was originally a 19th century foot and cattle trail. It's named after Kamehameha the Great's royal decree, the *Law of the Splintered Paddle*, which is included in the Hawai'i State Constitution;

> *The Law of the Splintered Paddle, Ke Kānāwai Māmalahoe, [as] decreed by Kamehameha I, [that] every elderly person, woman and child lie by the roadside in safety, shall be a unique and living symbol of the State's concern for public safety. The State shall have the power to provide for the safety of the people from crimes against persons and property.*

Essentially, it guarantees the safety of innocent bystanders. Kamehameha's original version was a little firmer; it ended - *Disobey, Die!*

Hula Daddy
Hula Daddy is arguably the best Kona Coffee in the world; they win all kinds of prizes for it, and the tour is the best I've seen. The word "artisanal" is over used, but it fits here. They grow, pick, sort, dry, roast, and package the coffee there, and it's all done by hand. The tour is small, you and a tour guide, takes as long as you like, and is interactive as all get out.

The roasting in particular is fascinating; it's done in very small batches, each one tasted and graded while the roast master explains every step and offers samples for tasting. One or both of the owners are generally on site and often are the tour guides. They have excellent free samples,

Coffee Country Tour

and you can sit and sip, looking out over Kailua Bay from what may be the best vantage point anywhere; binoculars are provided. Naturally, they'd like you to buy some coffee, and they'll ship anywhere for just the cost of postage, but you will not be embarrassed or held up to ridicule if you take the tour, sample the coffee and drive on. In general, this is true of all of the coffee tours.

Coffee Plantations

Actually, quite a few coffee plantations promote tours, but not all of them grow, dry, roast, and package coffee, or can handle drop-ins. Among those which do offer drop-in tours are (from north to south); UCC Hawaii, Holualoa Kona Coffee Company, Heavenly Hawaiian, and Greenwell Farms. More about Greenwell later.

49 Things to do on the Big Island

Something you will notice is that each one of the coffee farms has its own unique and colorful label. The annual Kona Coffee Festival in early November includes a competition for best label, as well as best coffees.

Holualoa

A little artsy town, strung out along the highway, with tons of art galleries and a good restaurant, Holuakoa Gardens and Cafe.

The name Holualoa means "long slide". Hawaiian nobles would ride wooden sleds down an earthen slideway covered with wet grass; the upper end of one such is near the town. The lower end is at the ocean near what is now Living Stones Church.

There is a road leading down the mountainside to the coast road just south of Holualoa, if you want to cut your trip short at this point.

Kuakini

Named after John Adams Kuakini, royal governor of Hawai'i Island when the first missionaries landed. He built the first church in Hawai'i, Mokuaikaua, in Kona, described in the Kailua Village tour.

Coffee Country Tour

Daifukuji Soto Mission

A 100 year old Buddhist temple, open to visitors. Park in front, on the grass, or behind the building. It is considered auspicious to drop spare pocket change in the box as you enter. The priest in residence may come out to greet you. If you go into the Kannon Shrine on the left, with the white carpet, please remove your shoes. Photos are ok.

Buddhism came to Hawai'i with Japanese laborers in the mid-19th century, and is now the second most common religion in Hawai'i.

Amy B. H. Greenwell Ethnobotanical Garden

The gardens have several acres of rare tropical plants, including plants indigenous to Hawai'i, with interpretative exhibits explaining their importance to early Hawaiians. There is a modest admission charge.

49 Things to do on the Big Island

Greenwell Farms

Greenwell is the largest family-owned coffee business in Hawai'i and dominates the world Kona coffee market. They buy beans from other farmers as well as growing their own. The tour is simpler than Hula Daddy's, but the samples are good. Try Kona Red, a delicious and healthful drink made from the formerly-discarded juice squeezed from the coffee berries.

Kealakekua Bay

Captain Cook made landfall in the bay in 1778 and was killed here in 1779. The bay is spectacularly beautiful, with great snorkeling and a pod of dolphins that makes its residence here. The dolphins apparently have no fear of humans. Parking is very limited, and entry into the water is difficult and dangerous except at the only actual beach, Manini Beach, which has about a dozen parking spots. If you do stop at Manini Beach, park completely off the roadway or you'll be towed very quickly.

There is limited parking (and restrooms) at Hikiau Heiau, an important historical landmark, where Napo'opo'o road ends. You can see the Captain Cook monument across the bay from this location.

Captain Cook

Captain James Cook discovered Hawai'i, or the Sandwich Islands, in 1778. He first made landfall at Waimea Bay on Kauai, but soon moved to Kealakekua Bay on Hawai'i

Coffee Country Tour

Island. He arrived during a period of celebration known as Makahiki; the Hawaiian new year festival in honor of the god Lono. The festival traditionally lasted four lunar months, from October or November through February or early March. It was celebrated with feasts and games, something like Thanksgiving, and conflict was forbidden during this period.

At first, Captain Cook and his crew got along quite well with the Hawaiians, but conflict arose over a "stolen" boat. When Cook and some crewmen went ashore to capture Hawaiian hostages against the return of the boat, he was killed.

The Hawaiians greatly respected Cook, and at first sought to treat his body as they would for of one of their

49 Things to do on the Big Island

nobility; strip the meat from the bones and inter the bones in a cave in the cliffs on the north shore of Kealakekua Bay. When the British protested this, the Hawaiians returned the body, which was buried at sea somewhere in the bay.

In 1878, when the present monument was erected marking the spot where Cook was killed, Queen Likelike donated the land on which the monument stands to England. The land around the monument is British territory today; about once a year, a British ship anchors in the Bay and a work party comes ashore to tidy up the monument.

The monument is reachable only by a strenuous 4 mile hike down a trail from the Mamalahoa Highway, near where Napo'opo'o Road meets the Highway; or by boat. In order to minimize wear to the monument area and the very delicate coral along the shoreline, a limited number of companies have permits from the State of Hawai'i to put visitors ashore on the monument grounds by boat or kayak. As a practical matter, anyone with the courage and stamina to paddle across the bay in a kayak is unlikely to be turned away.

It's easily a half-day excursion to paddle across the bay see the dolphins, hang out and snorkel at the monument, and paddle back. This is best done in the morning when it's calmest.

Pu'uhonua o Hōnaunau (Place of Refuge) National Historic Park

Hawaiians believed that persons who transgressed against their legal and religious system would be granted

Coffee Country Tour

amnesty if they made it to a place of refuge; this is one such place. It was also a royal residence. The National Park Service has restored and preserved the site and offers interpretative exhibits. There is a charge for parking and admission.

Immediately to the north of the park is a well-known snorkeling area known as "two step" because the easiest entry is by two steps in the rock. Snorkeling is great here, it's a marine wildlife preserve. Entry and exit can be a little tricky if there is a significant swell running. Check with the locals before venturing in. If there's nobody in the water, there's probably a reason. Actually, this is good advice in general.

St. Benedict›s Catholic Church (Painted Church)

This early Catholic church was moved to its present location in 1889. The interior is beautifully decorated in

49 Things to do on the Big Island

biblical scenes, painted in the 19th century by Father John Velge, an untrained but talented artist. It is badly in need of restoration. It is open to the public at no charge, but donations are welcomed and needed. This is a working church, with regularly scheduled mass.

Uchida Farm

A living history museum, complete with farm workers. There is an admission charge for this one. It authentically demonstrates what early coffee farming was like. The farmhouse is preserved as it would have been in the early 20th century including a farm "wife" who prepares midday lunch for the farm workers on the plantation. The farm workers are happy to demonstrate their trades.

Coffee Country Tour

49 Things to do on the Big Island

Northern Island Tour

Northern Island Tour

Get a free ukulele lesson, see The King, and other entertainment. Take a loop of the north end of the island through a couple of old sugar plantation towns, visit the only good sea port on the west side of the island, an ancient Hawaiian temple and an even older fishing village, and other interesting sights. It will take most of a day, depending on where you stop and for how long.

If you are staying on the west, or Kona side of the island, either in or near Kona or in one of the resorts north of Kona, head north following Highway 19, known as the Queen Ka'ahumanu Highway or the coast road. If you're on the Hilo side, you'll have to cross over either via the Saddle Road or along the Hamakua coast (more about this elsewhere).

Go to the "T" intersection near Kawaihae, about 9 miles north of the Waikoloa Road (the road that goes uphill to the right at a traffic light) and about 30 miles north of the Kona airport. At the "T" intersection, turn left onto Highway 270, past **Pu'ukohola National Historic Site** and **Spencer Beach Park**, followed within about a mile by the little port town of **Kawaihae** where you make a sharp right, still on 270. Head north about 20 miles, past all kinds of interesting things.

Very shortly after the turn, you pass the **Hamakua Macadamia Nut** factory; free samples. As you travel north to Hawi, notice how the vegetation changes abruptly from dry land brush to vivid green and fairly quickly to rain forest as you round the corner of the island onto the wind-

23

49 Things to do on the Big Island

ward side. The leeward, or down wind, side of this northern part of the island is sheltered by Kohala, one of the five volcanoes that make up the island.

One of the places you pass is **Lapakahi**, a semi-preserved ancient Hawaiian fishing village, complete with a self-guided tour of historic ruins and partly restored structures. It's hot and dusty, but a great photo opportunity.

There's a really nice visitors' welcome building at the extreme west end of **Hawi**, with the best restrooms you'll see in the area. The welcome center can provide you with all kinds of local information.

Leaving Hawi, you go along the fringes of a rain forest, passing **Saint Augustine Episcopal Church** on your left, one of the first Episcopal churches in Hawai'i. Stop in, the door is never locked and it's a lovely example of early Hawaiian churches. Be sure and close the door behind you to keep out stray cats and chickens.

The town of **Kapa'au** is the birthplace of Kamehameha the great, and a statue of the King is on the lawn of the town hall. There is quite a story about this statue. Kapa'au has a few galleries as well, including the fairly famous Ackerman Gallery. Naturally, there's a café across the street from the statue.

Traveling a little further, you pass a marked side road to the right that leads to **Kalahikiola Congregational Church**, built in 1855 and one of the first churches in Hawai'i. It's a pretty side trip.

The road dips down into a gulch, up the other side, and eventually just stops at the overlook to the **Pololu Valley**, a

24

Northern Island Tour

spectacularly scenic spot. The trail down into the valley is mud most of the time, and not well maintained. Enjoying the scenery from the overlook, however, is free and easy.

That's it; turn around and head back. In the center of downtown Kapa'au, find the "T" intersection with Highway 250. If you miss it, you can pick up Highway 250 again in Hawi.

Highway 250 takes you over **Kohala** at an elevation up to about 3500 ft., through forests and grassy grazing lands. Much of the cattle ranching on Hawai'i Island is in this area.

Again, there are several stopping places for photo opportunities. At some locations you can see most of the Kohala coast all the way down to Kailua-Kona on a clear day.

The road ends just outside of **Waimea**, a busy and prosperous upland town with, of course, its own share of galleries and restaurants, as well as being the home of two prestigious preparatory schools, Hawai'i Preparatory Academy and Parker School. You can either cut it short and return to the resort areas by turning right at the "T" intersection and following the road down the hill to Kawaihae, or you can turn left into Waimea town.

From Waimea, if you're staying in Kona you can head south on Highway 190. If you're staying at one of the resort areas north of Kona, drop down to the coast road either from Waimea to Kawaihae or at the Waikoloa Road, and go to your hotel from there.

49 Things to do on the Big Island

Northern Island Tour Points of Interest
Pu'ukohola National Historic Site

A "heiau" is a Hawaiian temple. They take many forms, depending on their intended use, ranging from simple stone piles to large, elaborate enclosed structures. Many were destroyed with the official end of the Hawaiian religion in 1819, but numerous examples remain. Pu'ukohola is one such. The National Park Service maintains it and furnishes interpretative exhibits. There is no charge for admission.

Pu'ukohola Heiau was built by Kamehameha the Great in 1791 after he was told by a priest to build a temple to gain the favor of the war god, Kuka'iliimoka, in order to fulfill the prophecy that he, Kamehameha, would unite the islands under his rule. The temple is built of fitted stones, without mortar, typical of Hawaiian stone construction, and took about a year to complete. It was probably dedi-

Northern Island Tour

cated with one or more human sacrifices. Supposedly, stones were passed hand-to-hand from the Pololu Valley over a distance of about 14 miles. According to legend, Kamehameha himself broke sacred law by physically participating in the construction of the Heiau. Kamehameha did succeed in his dream of uniting all the islands, the first to do so.

Note that Pu'ukohola is built on the site of an earlier Heiau, Mailekini, visible below and in front of Pu'ukohola when seen from the makai, or seaward, side. Further to the west of the heiau and below it are the remains of Hale O Kapuni Heiau, submerged in the inlet just below Pu'ukohola and not normally visible. This heiau is sacred to sharks and the shark god, Kāmohoali'i; sharks are common in the inlet.

The heiau itself is still used by practitioners of the Hawaiian religion, presumably without human sacrifices these days. At the entrance to the heiau itself you will see crossed sticks with what appear to be balls at the upper ends; this is the traditional sign that an area is "*kapu*", or forbidden.

You can take about a ½ mile walking tour of the site, looping around the seaward side of Pu'ukohola Heiau, down to the shore, then back up again.

Spencer Beach Park

Spencer Beach Park is a quiet, protected beach with lots of shade. It has a shallow, sandy bottom, a lifeguard, showers, restrooms, shade, and lots of parking. It is a good beach for children and picnics, but not good for snorkeling.

49 Things to do on the Big Island

From Spencer Beach you can walk south either along the old paved road leading south from the parking lot, or along the Ala Kahakai trail, marked by a labeled post, leading through the trees next to the shore and just south of the pavilion at the south end of the beach. The Ala Kahakai trail is rough in spots. It is part of a 175-mile trail system around the west and south sides of the island.

About ½ mile south of Spencer Beach is Maumai Beach; no facilities, but great snorkeling. It's a relatively flat, sandy beach, well protected from the open ocean, largely unvisited and moderately difficult to reach. The very small parking area on the road above the beach only has about 5 spaces and is controlled by the Mauna Kea Beach Resort, so on a typical day you will find only a few other users, generally locals. Worth the hike if you want a pretty, secluded beach.

Kawaihae

Kawaihae is the only decent port on the west side of Hawai'i Island. It's pretty small, and is served mainly by daily barges from Honolulu. A significant portion of the imports of food and goods come to Hawai'i Island through this port.

There's not much to see, since the port area itself is restricted access, but you can travel to the end of the paved road and admire the outer harbor. You might see a barge arriving or leaving in tow. Once a month or so the military will bring in a landing ship to beach in the inner harbor as a training exercise. If you walk out on the breakwater, pay very close attention to the state of the sea; waves will some-

Northern Island Tour

times go completely over the breakwater. It is very dangerous in anything but the best weather.

Hamakua Macadamia Nut Factory

Just mauka (inland) from Highway 270 and about ¼ mile north of Kawaihae is the Hamakua Macadamia Nut Company's factory store, about 500 yards off the highway up a steep drive. This is a fascinating place for big and little kids to see the packing operation, safely protected behind glass walls. You can also eat yourself sick on samples, including some "I dare you to eat this" flavors.

Lapakahi State Historical Park

This is a preserved Hawaiian fishing village, probably first established in the 14th century and occupied right up into the early 20th century. You can pick up a brochure at

49 Things to do on the Big Island

the little visitors' center and take a self-guided tour of the ruins. There is one restored building and a couple of partly restored ones, and the rest is mostly stone ruins. The ocean is spectacularly beautiful at this location. It can be a good snorkeling spot for experts, in calm weather. There are porta-potties here as well.

Hawi

Hawi is a former sugar plantation town. Much of the north end of the island was once planted in sugar cane. The cane was then hauled to sugar mills where the juice was squeezed out and cooked down into sugar. The old plantation

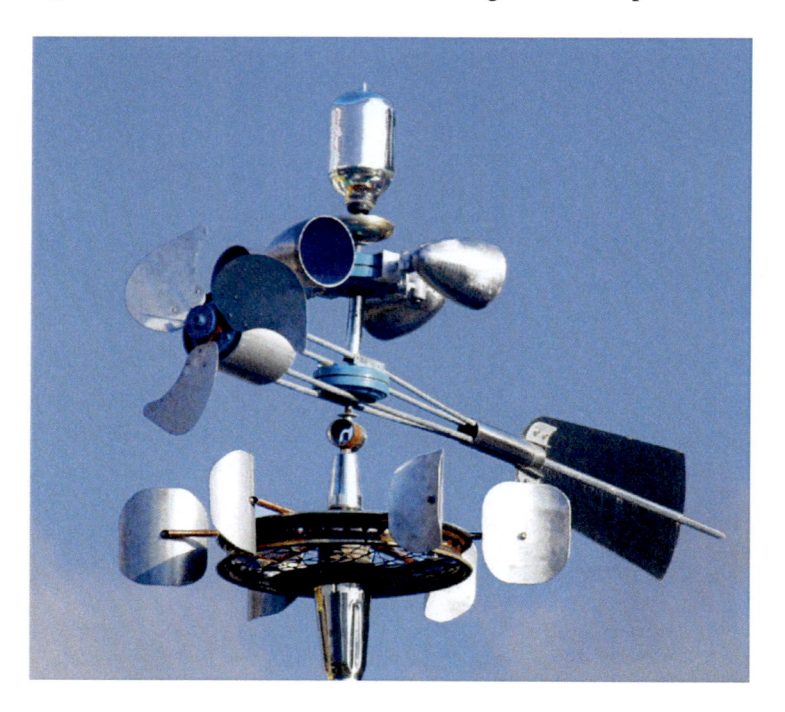

Northern Island Tour

towns, including Hawi and nearby Kapa'au, grew up near the plantations to provide services to workers. The plantations are now gone, and the towns have become quiet backwaters.

The visitors' center as you approach Hawi offers good restrooms and information. Park anywhere; all of Hawi is within walking distance.

Like seemingly everywhere in Hawai'i, Hawi has its share of art galleries, t-shirt shops, restaurants, and general tourist-y stuff. One attraction is Hawi Gallery, on the right as you enter town, which specializes in ukulele sales. Prices range from about $100 up into the stratosphere, and they're happy to give a free lesson or two to anyone who asks. They also have a good selection of vintage Hawaiian shirts.

One unique feature in Hawi is the whirlagigs on top of some of the buildings. Made from junk, they spin in the wind for no reason other than fun.

A little further on are assorted stores and a really nice café/ice cream parlor, the Kohala Coffee Mill. Have some Tropical Dreams ice cream, made locally in Waimea. It is excellent, with unusual tropical flavors. Also notable is a clothing store, As Hawi Turns. Right in front of it is the official turn-around point for the 112-mile bicycle leg of the annual Ironman World Championship, held on Hawai'i Island each year in early October. The highway is closed to traffic for most of race day to accommodate the athletes.

Across the street is Bamboo, a restaurant in a lightly renovated former bordello and/or hotel. Bamboo has good local food, including local, grass-fed, beef, and an interesting history.

49 Things to do on the Big Island

Saint Augustine Episcopal Church

Christian missionaries first came to Hawai'i from New England in 1820. These first missionaries succeeded in convincing the Hawaiians to keep missionaries representing other sects from proselytizing in Hawai'i until 1839, when Kamehameha III issued the Edict of Toleration, allowing missionaries of all religions to come to Hawai'i. In about 1866 Kamehameha IV invited the first Episcopal missionaries. St. Augustine Church was built in 1884 to serve English families who had migrated to the area to work on the sugar plantations, and as merchants to provide services to the residents. The beautiful wooden altar was shipped around the Horn from England. The original building was expanded in 1913 into its present cross shape, but the front part is as built in the 19th century.

Northern Island Tour

The church is always unlocked, and visitors are welcomed. It is in a spectacularly photogenic location.

Kapa'au

Kapa'au is home to a famous statue of Kamehameha the Great. If you are a fan of television shows about Hawai'i you've probably seen such a statue in front of a Honolulu building, supposedly the headquarters of a fictional police agency. The Honolulu statue is a copy. The ship carrying the original statue

49 Things to do on the Big Island

from France to Hawai'i sunk off the Falkland Islands. Since the statue was insured, the Hawaiian legislature, which had paid for the statue, ordered a copy to be made. This copy is the statue in Honolulu. Meanwhile, the original was salvaged and sold to the town of Kapa'au, where it is installed today.

On Kamehameha Day, June 11, a state holiday, the statue is bedecked with leis and offerings and there are parades everywhere. Kamehameha the Great was the first king to unite all of the Hawaiian Islands, creating for the first time a unified nation, He is revered everywhere in Hawai'i.

Northern Island Tour

Kalahikiola Congregational Church

This is one of the first half-dozen churches built in Hawai'i. It was severely damaged in an earthquake, but has been restored to its original condition. The church was built in 1855 by Elias Bond, who also built a nearby school, and started the first sugar plantation in the area. The plantation workers were treated exceptionally well by the prevailing standards of the time. The surrounding area is known as the Bond District. The descendants of Reverend Bond still own much of it.

Pololu Valley

Pololu Valley was formed by erosion and landslides on the northern slope of Kohala. It is one of three valleys on the north shore: Waipio on the east, Pololu on the west, and the nearly unreachable Waimanu in the middle. The trail drops to the valley floor by about 600 ft. in about ½ mile. At the bottom you can cross the shallow Pololu River to a black sand beach. There are no facilities, but if you're in good shape, hiking down the trail will take you to a bit of paradise. Be sure and bring drinking water, wear your hiking boots, and watch out for slippery areas. The bottom is privately owned farmland, so stick to the established trail.

The river is fed by agricultural runoff and is not safe to drink from. The ocean here is extremely dangerous, so unless you're a really experienced open water swimmer, it's best to stay out.

If you're feeling only a tiny bit adventuresome, hike down the trail a few hundred yards to about the second

49 Things to do on the Big Island

switchback; it's probably the best photo vista of the valley. You'll know it when you see it.

Kohala

Hawai'i Island consists of five big volcanoes; Kohala, Mauna Kea, Mauna Loa, Hualalai, and Kilauea. Kohala, the oldest and long extinct, was once covered in sandalwood trees, cut down in the early 19th century and sold to China to pay the Kingdom's debt for Western arms and machinery. Now, it's prime grazing land for sheep and cattle, lush and green on the upper slopes. The road across the upper slopes of Kokala was the original access road to Hawi; the coast road was built sometime later.

Waimea

Waimea is the center of the Hawaiian cattle industry and home to Parker Ranch, once the largest contiguous ranch in the Unite States. One of the sights of Waimea is the statue of Ikea Purdy, a Hawaiian cowboy, who won the Rodeo World Championship in 1908, surprising just about everybody except Hawaiians. You will see his successors in Waimea, real working cowboys, just about the muddiest and dirtiest anywhere.

Cattle raising is a major industry on Hawai'i Island dating back to the very early 19th century, the time of Kamehameha the Great. Lord George Vancouver brought the first cattle to Hawai'i in about 1803. Most, but not all, of the cattle raised in Hawai'i are shipped to the mainland as year-

Northern Island Tour

lings to fatten up in Texas and California. Most of them ship out of Kawaihae in special containers on a 9-day voyage to California. A few travel by air in specially modified jets.

The cattle that remain in Hawai'i are raised to adulthood on the slopes of Kohala and the flatter grasslands to the east. The locally raised grass-fed beef is a delicacy; you can frequently enjoy it at some local restaurants or buy it in grocery stores. Most Americans are accustomed to the taste and texture of corn-fed cattle, raised in feedlots. Grass-fed cattle can be tougher and have a slightly different taste. Enjoy the difference!

49 Things to do on the Big Island

Northeast Tour - The Hamakua Coast

Northeast Tour - The Hamakua Coast

Cross the island to the old port town of Hilo, round the northern part of the island through rain forests, with a possible side trip to the two tallest mountains in the world (as measured from their bases on the sea floor). This is probably going to take most of a day.

From either the Kohala Coast resort area or the Kona area, go to the intersection of the Mamalahoa Highway with the **Saddle Road**, Highway 200. The intersection is 3 miles south of the intersection of the Mamalahoa Highway and the Waikoloa Road, and about 20 miles north of Kona.

At about the halfway point on the Saddle Road, on the north side is the **Mauna Kea Recreation Area**. A few miles further on is a **cinder cone** on the right, rising about 300 feet and covered with vegetation. At that point there is a road on the left of the Saddle Road leading north, up Mauna Kea. **The Mauna Kea Visitor's Center** is up this road at an elevation of 9200 feet.

Just slightly further on, beyond the cinder cone, is the access road to **Mauna Loa.** It's marked as access to the weather observatory. The first few hundred feet of the road are rough but passable, after which it improves to a narrow but smooth, winding, one-lane road all the way to the weather observatory located at about 11,000 feet elevation.

The Saddle Road is almost 60 miles long, measured from the Mamalahoa Highway to downtown **Hilo**. The last few miles of the Saddle Road wind through a thinly-populated residential area.

49 Things to do on the Big Island

As you approach Hilo, you can either turn left on marked Highway 200, Waianuenue Avenue, which leads to an intersection with Highway 19 near the north end of town; or continue to the "T" intersection and turn right, then immediately left at West Pu'ainako Street, downhill eventually to join Highway 19 near the south end of town.

Many historic buildings are along Kamehameha Avenue, which runs north and south, paralleling the waterfront and Highway 19. Parking here can be tricky to find.

To leave Hilo, head north on Highway 19, the familiar Mamalahoa Highway.

About 5 miles north of town you will come to a fork, with the "historic" Mamalahoa Highway branching to the right. Take that right fork, it's very pretty and doesn't add much time to the trip (unless, of course, you stop). It winds through a dense tropical rain forest, with spectacular scenery and a couple of botanical gardens along the way.

The turnoff to **Akaka Falls** is about 10 miles north of Hilo along the historic Mamalahoa Highway (Highway 19).

The road parallels the sea as it rounds the north end of the island, passing by or through former sugar towns like Lapahoehoe, with it's famous railroad museum; and **Honoka'a**. Beautiful road, spectacular scenery, the old Hawai'i. Very pretty. Top down country if you have a convertible and it's not raining.

At about mile marker 35 you'll pass Kalopa Road. About 3 or 4 miles mauka (inland) of the highway is **Kalopa State Recreation Area**, a forest preserve with hiking trails, cabins, and camp sites.

Northeast Tour - The Hamakua Coast

If you get off the Mamalahoa Highway at **Honoka'a** to your right at about mile marker 40, you can continue through town to the **Waipio Overlook**, about 10 miles farther along the coast on Highway 240.

Back on the Mamalahoa Highway leaving Honoka'a you drive through cattle country and forest to the town of **Waimea**.

From Waimea you can either continue south on the Mamalahoa Highway to Kona, or go west to Kawaihae, the most active seaport on the west side of the island and location of Spencer Beach and Pu'ukohola Heiau, described in the Northern Loop tour.

Hamakua Coast Tour Points of Interest
Saddle Road

Hawaiians avoided the saddle between Mauna Kea and Mauna Loa, as they believe it was a place where the gods fought. During WW II the US Army built a "short cut" road between the east and west sides of the island across the saddle between the two mountains. The original road between Kona and Hilo was a rough one-lane road, portions of which are still usable. The road rises to about 6500 ft. and has some amazing and unearthly scenery, when it's not shrouded in clouds. The saddle is also the site of Pohakuloa Training Area, a US Army training installation.

49 Things to do on the Big Island

The old road was pretty bad. You can pick up a segment of the old, narrow road about 5 miles north of the Waikoloa road on the Mamalahoa Highway. It's paved, narrow, and with several one-lane bridges.

Because of the high altitude of the Saddle Road, this drive is not a good idea if you plan to go SCUBA diving in the next day or so.

If you drive up either Mauna Kea or Mauna Loa, be aware of the high altitude. Both top out at about 14,000 ft; this is close to the altitude where airplane pilots need supplementary oxygen. Symptoms of altitude sickness include exhaustion, loss of consciousness, and general malaise.

Mauna Kea Recreation Area

It's a convenient pit stop, with a small playground, some cabins and camping spaces to rent, and the only restrooms along the saddle road.

Cinder Cone

This is a bioisland, an isolated biome surrounded by a newer lava flow. The vegetation and small animal life on the elevated cinder cone survived being surrounded by the new lava flow and helped to re-vegetate and re-populate the new lava flow as it weathers.

You will also see a small rock altar just before you get to the turnoff; this is a place where Hawaiians make offerings before venturing up the mountainside.

Northeast Tour - The Hamakua Coast

Mauna Kea Visitor's Center

Mauna Kea is the tallest mountain in the world, if you count the part that is underwater. It rises about 20,000 ft. from the sea floor, then about another 14,000 ft. to its summit. It sometimes snows on Mauna Kea. The summit of Mauna Kea is home to more than a dozen astronomical observatories, including the world's largest, the twin 10-meter Keck telescopes, visible from more than half of the total island surface.

From the Saddle Road you can drive up to the visitor's center at an elevation of 9200 ft. Travel beyond that usually takes 4WD, and visitors are not especially welcome at the telescopes themselves. The only observatory with regular public access is Keck, which has an observation deck and flushing toilets. It is really windy and cold at the summit, and the air is thin. You have to really want to do this.

49 Things to do on the Big Island

In the winter, it snows on Mauna Kea a few times a year. Hawaiians used to climb up and slide down the snowy slopes, which is quite an undertaking. Now, it is pretty common on snow days to see trucks loaded with snow, headed to Kona, Waimea, or Hilo so the kids can play in the snow.

If the sky is clear, there will be telescopes set up at the visitor's center to view the sun during the daytime, and celestial objects at night. It's free, but be aware that this is a seriously high elevation and it can be cold at night. By the way, the road up is steep, a 25% grade in places. You might want to schedule a trip to the visitor's center as a separate excursion. Well worth it if you're an amateur astronomer.

Mauna Loa

Mauna Loa is only about 400 ft shorter than Mauna Kea. There is a weather observatory at about 11,000 ft el-

Northeast Tour - The Hamakua Coast

evation, where the paved road ends. At about the 10,000 ft level you pass a scientific experiment observing high energy cosmic rays. From there, the hardy can hike an additional 3 or 4 miles to the summit; be prepared for cold, thin air, and possible dense fog. Or, just have a picnic at the end of the paved road and enjoy the amazing view from a point higher than most small aircraft fly.

By the way, Mauna Loa, like the rest of the Hawaiian volcanoes, is a typical shield volcano. It is technically still active, although it hasn't erupted in a few centuries. Shield volcanoes are deceptive in size because of their gentle slope. The lava erupts from a shield volcano in a smooth, relatively slow flow, spreading over a large area, rather than a violent explosive flow as from, for instance, Mount St. Helens. Mauna Loa is the most massive volcano on earth; it is so massive that the earth's crust is depressed beneath it by a few miles. Mauna Loa, like Mauna Kea, rests on the sea floor about 20,000 ft below sea level.

Hilo

Hilo is the county seat and an old seaport. Most of the buildings along the waterfront were damaged by the 1946 tsunami, but everything has been restored. Park along Kamehameha Avenue and walk around. You can walk over to the waterfront itself, but it's not a very good beach. There are some good restaurants near the waterfront in Hilo. You can also park on Banyan Drive, at the south end of Hilo Bay, and visit the beautiful Queen Lili'uokalani Gardens.

49 Things to do on the Big Island

The banyan trees along the roadside were planted by various celebrities, identified by small plaques. This is where the few big-ish hotels in Hilo are located.

A few blocks mauka from the waterfront you can find the old town square and Haile Street Church, another of the first churches built in Hawai'i.

Hilo has lots of great museums; the Lyman Museum at 276 Haile Street, the Imiloa Astronomy Center, a spectacular museum dedicated to Hawaiian astronomy and navigation located at 600 'Imiloa Place, and the Pacific Tsunami Museum, at the north end of Kamehameha Avenue. There are good restaurants in Hilo, and fun shopping in the old portion of town, near the waterfront.

Northeast Tour - The Hamakua Coast

49 Things to do on the Big Island

Akaka Falls

It's a half-mile loop trail to see the 400+ ft. waterfall, and you're surrounded by beautiful tropical foliage. It's a nice stop along the way. Plan on an hour or so to drive in, park, walk to the vantage point, take pictures, etc. There is a $5/car fee for non-residents.

Kalopa State Recreation Area

Kalopa State Recreation Area just east of Honaka'a on the Hawai'i Belt Road is an excellent family destination. It's well developed, with restrooms and shelters, and a couple of really spectacular hiking trails. The 3/4 mile nature trail is family-friendly. Follow the signs, it's about 3 miles off the Belt Road between the 39 and 40 mile markers, on marked roads. You will think you're lost as you wander seemingly forever along winding roads past scattered homes and farms, but eventually you'll get to the Recreation Area.

The trails are for the most part well marked and reasonably well maintained, but you might encounter lots of mud, rocks, and brush; they are by no stretch of the imagination ADA-accessible. It is a rain forest, so be prepared for rain. It's beautiful rain or shine. If you want to see some tropical rain forest close up, this is it.

Honoka'a

Another former sugar town, now enjoying new growth. The People's Theatre on the main street hosts famous performers from all over the world in a surprisingly modest

Northeast Tour - The Hamakua Coast

venue. There are several good restaurants in Honoka'a. The Tex Drive in, right off the Mamalahoa Highway, is famous for its malasadas, a sweet filled pastry of Portuguese origin, resembling a jelly donut.

Many Portuguese came to Hawai'i in the late 19th century to work on the sugar plantations and cattle ranches. The Portuguese influence appears especially strong in Honoka'a; Grandma's Kitchen, on Long Soup Corner (yes, it's marked that way) boasts of the Portuguese origin of its food. The distinctive local accent has a trace of Portuguese in it.

Waipio Valley

At the northern end of Hawai'i Island on the slopes of Kohala are (from east to west) Waipio, Waimanu, and Pololu Valleys. The surrounding terrain is at an elevation of 2000 or more feet; these valleys are cut into the lava to sea level by landslides and have flowing streams and waterfalls from rain and snow on the high elevations of Kohala. These valleys are the ancient homes of kings, and in Captain Cook's time, many thousands of people. In 1780 in the Waipio Valley Kamehameha had a vision of the war god Kukailimoku in which he was proclaimed, correctly as it turned out, future ruler of all the islands.

Today, the valley is entirely private property. There are essentially no urban services; no power, water, or waste services other than what the small number of inhabitants provide themselves. No paved roads, for that matter. The inhabitants raise taro and vegetables; some work in the surrounding communities above the valleys. Habitations in

49 Things to do on the Big Island

the valleys were severely damaged in the 1946 tsunami, which essentially destroyed all structures. Most residents left, leaving behind livestock. The Waipio is now home to a number of short, wild horses descended from those abandoned in 1946 and later. One of the popular commercial activities is horseback riding in Waipio Valley, which is fun, although you might be as tall as the horse.

You can walk down into the Waipio along the paved road, it's a 25% grade in places, descending about 800 feet over a distance of a few miles. You also get to walk back up, which is quite a climb. If this doesn't seem like fun, there are a number of tour operators ready to drive you down and back. Or, you can just look at it from the observation point.

Waimea

Waimea is the center of the cattle industry and home to Parker Ranch, at one time the second largest ranch in the United States. Waimea is proud of its heritage, home of the paniolo, or Hawaiian cowboy. Some weekends you might see a rodeo at the grounds just south of Waimea. Hawaiian grass fed beef is a delicacy.

Northeast Tour - The Hamakua Coast

49 Things to do on the Big Island

See a Volcano - Southern Tour

See a Volcano - Southern Tour

This is a long trip, and generally a big island must-do. You can either go south along the Mamalahoa Highway (Highway 19), around Southpoint, and north to Hawai'i Volcanoes National Park, or go to Hilo and south (see Saddle Road, below and in the Hamakua Coast route), which is slightly faster but bypasses a few things. Both routes are well marked. Either way, it's a full day, 4 or 5 driving hours, and about 200 miles. Here is the southern route. It partly duplicates the southern loop tour and the Hamakua Coast loop.

Go south on the Mamalahoa Highway, Highway 19. If you're staying on the Kohala coast it's slightly faster to take the coast road, the Queen Ka'ahumanu Highway (Queen K), to Kona, than the Mamalahoa Highway. The Queen K joins the Mamalahoa near Kealakekua, from where it's more than 90 miles to Hawai'i Volcanoes National Park. The new road is Highway 11.

You will pass some of the sights on the southern loop tour, including Napo'opo'o Road and Pu'uhonua o Honaunau. At about mile marker 90 or so you pass **Ho'okena Beach Park**. A little farther on is Hawaiian Ocean View Estates (HOVE), the largest subdivision in the nation at 18 square miles. It is probably the least expensive land in Hawai'i.

The turnoff to **Southpoint** is at about mile marker 68, Southpoint Road. The town of Na'alehu is a little farther on. At about mile marker 58 is **Punalu'u Beach Park**.

49 Things to do on the Big Island

The road climbs through increasingly-forested terrain to a dense rain forest at **Hawaiian Volcanoes National Park**. It is a National Park and has a modest entry fee. This is usually a must-do for visitors to the big island. You can find good restaurants in the nearby town of Volcano.

Traveling north from the Park on Highway 11 about 15 miles you pass Akatsuka Orchid Gardens, with spectacular orchids on display and for sale. About 25 miles from the Park, past the town of Kurtistown, you come to Kea'au and the junction with Highway 130, the only entryway to the Pahoa District, with **Ahalanui Park** and Kahena Black Sand Beach. It's a good 30 miles off Highway 11 to these attractions.

Hilo is only a short distance north of Kea'au. From there, the Saddle Road (Highway 200) will return you to West Hawai'i.

Southern Tour Points of Interest
Ho'okena Beach Park

The beach is a mix of black volcanic sand and white coral sand; it has an interesting greyish-black color. It's a broad, sandy beach with restrooms and some shade, and kayak and boogie board rentals. You can camp on the beach for a small fee. It was a small harbor at one time, and the remnants of the old pier can be seen.

See a Volcano - Southern Tour

Southpoint

This is the southern-most point in the United States. As with most of the southern shore, it is rough and rocky. This is because it is relatively new land, being of recent volcanic origin. The actual road to Southpoint and the green sand beach (not a good swimming spot) is rough, 4WD territory; locals will take you there to look and admire the green (actually, olive-colored) sand.

Punalu'u Beach Park

Punalu'u Beach Park is a rocky, rough black sand beach frequented by endangered turtles, seals, and birds. The black sand is the result of hot lava from Kilauea entering the water and exploding. The Punalu'u area has several an-

49 Things to do on the Big Island

cient heiaus, or stone temple structures dating from about 1100 CE. It is also the birthplace of Henry Opukahai'a, the orphaned Hawaiian boy who encouraged the missionaries to come to Hawai'i.

Hawai'i Volcanoes National Park

This is really what you came for. Kilauea, the only currently active volcano in the United States, has been erupting continuously since 1983. It is now part of Hawai'i Volcanoes National Park, which has a small admission fee. The park is at the southeast corner of the Island, and takes about 4 hours to reach from Kona, going around the south end of the island, if you don't stop for much; about 3 hours if you go the other way, through Hilo. You can visit the Jagger Observatory overlooking the crater with a nice view of Mauna Loa from the south, walk through an underground lava tube located in a rain forest, and see steam rising out of the ground. It's safe and interesting. The best view of the crater is from the dining room of the Volcano House, the hotel/restaurant on the Park grounds. The food there demonstrates the truth of the adage that places with a good view do not need to exert themselves in the food department, but it's the only game around, so... Besides, kids of all ages love this; the view through the picture windows and the walk behind the hotel is astounding. Fortunately, for safety's sake, you cannot actually get close to flowing lava.

Chain of Craters Road winds down to the cliffs overlooking the sea, ending abruptly at a fairly fresh lava flow. The round trip easily takes an hour. The County Highway Department has been at work re-opening the blocked end

See a Volcano - Southern Tour

of the road as an alternate route to the Pahoa area, on the eastern tip of the island, which was recently threatened by lava flows from Kileaua. The lava flow would have cut off the only road into the Pahoa district, Highway 130. When Chain of Craters Road is re-opened it will be possible to follow the coast through Pahoa, then to Hilo.

Near where Chain of Craters Road makes a left, southerly turn at the bottom of the hill you can see a rock arch carved in the cliffs if you (carefully!) look to your right from near the edge of the cliff, where there is a scenic lookout. The cliffs are steep, tall, rocky at the bottom, and pounded relentlessly by the surf. If this sounds like a dangerous place, it is.

Hiking trails abound, at skill levels for all. One of the more strenuous hiking trails leads to the Mauna Loa summit. The Park Service estimates that this is a 4-day hike for the very fit, and is highly dangerous because of potential

49 Things to do on the Big Island

fast-changing weather conditions and a lack of water and shelter along the route.

In 1824, as a demonstration of her new Christian faith, High Chieftess Kapi'olani recited a Christian prayer, then entered the Halema'uma'u crater. Pele did not kill her, an event commemorated in a poem by Alfred, Lord Tennyson, "Kapiolani". Nonetheless, Kilauea remains vigorously active.

Ahalanui Park

Ahalanui is a natural hot spring, bigger than an Olympic swimming pool. The water is bathtub warm, and there are showers, tables, and restrooms at the park and at nearby Isaac Hale Beach Park, MacKenzie State Recreation Area, and Kahena Black Sand Beach. The water is about 6 to 8 feet deep, with no shallows, so it's not good for non-swimmers. It's partly improved and man-made so there are easy entry/exit places.

Hilo

Hilo is the largest town on Hawai'i Island and can be tricky to navigate. There are some suggestions of things to do in the Hamakua Coast Tour. If you just want to get home, there are three routes back to West Hawai'i.

- Straight up Kamehameha Avenue and Highway 19 to Highway 200, Waianuenue Avenue, which leads

See a Volcano - Southern Tour

to the Saddle Road. This route takes you all the way through town along the waterfront, but it's not that long a trip and it's the easiest to follow.

- Left at Highway 11, then right at Pu'ainako Street, then left again on Highway 200, the Saddle Road.
- Continue on Kamehameha Avenue and Highway 19, through town and return via the Hamakua Coast. This is the longest route, and the most scenic, but it makes for a really long day.

49 Things to do on the Big Island

Kailua-Kona History Tour

Kailua-Kona History Tour

Lucky you! Hawai'i Island is blessed with many reminders of Hawai'i's history. If you're in Kona with an hour or so to spare, take this short walking tour of several historic sites. Park in the free lot on the north side of Hualalai Road, near Ali'i Drive, or in the free lot just off the Kuakini Highway, south of Palani Road. Visit the first Christian church, Kamehameha's personal temple, and a royal palace.

Start at **Mokuaikaua Church**, almost at the far north end of Ali'i Drive where it makes a turn around Kailua Bay. Mokuaikaua Church is the first church in Hawai'i.

Across the street is the **Hulihe'e Palace**, a former royal residence and now a museum. There is a charge for admission, but you can wander the grounds for free.

South a bit and crossing the street again is Kona Marketplace, a shopping center. All the way in the back, near the restrooms, is an old stone hitching post marking the site of the **first Catholic mass** on Hawai'i Island.

Back up the street again and around the curve to the grounds of the King Kamehameha Kona Beach Hotel is **Ahu'ena Heiau**, King Kamehameha's personal temple. The sandy beach in front of the hotel is probably where the first missionaries landed.

Kailua Pier is the starting point for the World Championship **Ironman Triathlon**; not quite a historic site, but interesting nonetheless to the athletes in the family.

49 Things to do on the Big Island

Kailua-Kona History Tour
Points of Interest
Mokuaikaua Church

In 1819 Kamehameha II decreed an end to the old religious and social structure based on kapu. In 1820, not knowing of this change in the social structure, the first Christian missionaries arrived in Hawai'i. They built quite a few churches, mostly patterned on the New England churches with which they were familiar. Mokuaikaua Church, at the north end of Ali'i Drive just across from Kailua Pier, was the first Christian church in Hawai'i. It is a working church with regular services, but visitors are wel-

Kailua-Kona History Tour

come to drop in during the day and evening to see the historical exhibits. There is usually a docent to explain things and offer insights. It's also free.

Hulihe'e Palace

The Hulihe'e Palace, across Ali'i Drive from Mokuaikaua Church, was the residence of the Royal Governor of Hawai'i Island. It is now a museum, complete with early 19th century furnishings. There is a fee for entry, but you can wander the grounds for free.

First Catholic Mass

Until the 1839 Edict of Toleration, the only missionaries allowed in Hawai'i were the Congregationalist missionaries sent by the American Board of Commissioners for Foreign Missions, in New England. After the Edict came missionaries of other sects, including previously-forbidden Catholic missionaries. The location of the first mass on Hawai'i Island is marked by a stone hitching post located within a small strip mall south of Mokuaikaua Church, Kona Marketplace. It is towards the back and somewhat indecorously next to the restrooms. About a half mile south of this spot is St. Michael the Archangel Church, a new church built on the site of the original and a worthwhile sight in itself. The water pond in front of St. Michael's is the site of the original spring supplying water to the village of Kailua-Kona.

49 Things to do on the Big Island

Ahu'ena Heiau

This heiau is also located just off Ali'i Drive at its very north end, on the grounds of the King Kamehameha Kona Beach Hotel and across Kailua Bay from the Hulihe'e Palace and Mokuaikaua Church. It was the personal temple of King Kamehameha I, who died at this spot in 1819. Ironically, in 1820 the first Christian missionaries were granted permission to come ashore at the adjacent beach, next to the Hulihe'e Palace.

The present structure is an accurate reconstruction of the original heiau, based on contemporaneous drawings and documents, and was built in the 1970's. The original heiau and stone platform extended somewhat further east and were partly demolished long ago to make way for Kailua Pier.

Kailua-Kona History Tour

The heiau is dedicated to Lono, God of peace, agriculture, and prosperity. The light colored structure resembling a chimney is the Anu'u, or oracle tower, where priests received prophesies from the gods. Anu'u were only built at the heiaus of rulers. Also visible are a number of Ki'i Akua, or carved wooden temple images of gods.

Ironman Triathlon

It's not really a historic spot, but it's interesting all the same. The annual Ironman Triathlon, which happens during the second weekend in October, came to the Big Island in 1981. It's supposedly the outcome of an argument among athletes about who's event was the hardest; swimming, bicycling, or running. The decision; do them all! It's a 2.4 mile open-water swim in Kailua Bay, a 112 mile bicycle ride to Hawi and back, and a full marathon, 26+ miles. These may be the finest athletes in the world. The start/transition/end point is right there on Ali'i Drive, next to Kailua Pier.

49 Things to do on the Big Island

Other Fun Things

Other Fun Things

Have a Picnic

Actually, this can be combined with most of the other things to do; have a picnic at the beach, pack a picnic for your expedition to Mauna Loa, and so on. The trick is to make the picnic packing as easy and fun as possible.

You can, of course, just take the easy way out and stop at Subway or another fast food chain; nothing wrong with that, but we can do a little better with minimal effort. Look no farther than the nearest grocery store.

Most of the grocery stores make good-to-great deli sandwiches, and probably have an array on the shelf. As a general rule, the nice lady behind the deli counter will be happy to custom build you a sandwich for about $5 that'll knock your socks off.

Sushi; easy choice! Again, grocery stores generally have a sushi chef in house; it's fresh and well done. You might have to ask for extra soy sauce; it seems to be somehow valuable.

For fancy stuff, grocery stores with a more visitor-oriented client base nearly always have an array of fried chicken, salads, spring rolls, and the like. Foodland and KTA are two chains that generally have a wide variety of picnic-suitable foods. Safeway is an old standby as well.

While you're at it you can pick up candy bars, chips, drinks, and whatever; one-stop picnic shopping. You can even get a bag to carry it all in. In fact, you have to; single-use plastic bags are banned on Hawai'i Island except for

49 Things to do on the Big Island

specific purposes such as separating ice cream or meat from the rest of your groceries. A reuseable grocery bag will set you back about $1.

You might try some Hawaiian specialties while you're at it. Poke (pronounced po-kay) is diced fish with spices; delicious, if you like sushi and sashimi. Malasadas are sweet chunks of fried dough, often filled like a jelly donut.

Naturally, you want some place to sit, right? While some beaches and most of the parks have benches or chaise lounges, they're pretty popular and in the case of the benches, anchored in place. If your condo isn't stocked with folding chairs, drop by Lowes, Home Depot, K-Mart, Target, or Walmart and pick up beach chairs. You can generally find fairly basic canvas and aluminum chairs that fit into a carrying bag for less than $10, and you'll use them over and over. These are the ones where the whole thing collapses into a roughly cylindrical shape. When you leave, either leave them in the condo for the next people or drop them at a thrift store. The expensive Tommy Bahama folding chairs with the built in bags and pouches are nice, and might be a bit more comfy, but cost a lot more and are surprisingly clumsy to carry; the inexpensive chairs fit easily over the shoulder and weigh next to nothing. They won't last more than a season, but what do you care?

Fold-up umbrellas and sun shelters are nice, but heavy and awkward and, in the case of the less expensive umbrellas, prone to blow away. Those trade winds and sea breezes can get pretty strong. It's easier to look for natural shade.

Other Fun Things

49 Things to do on the Big Island

Other Fun Things

See Hula

And other things, too. The resort complexes offer a variety of free entertainment; check the on-line calendars for Queen's Marketplace (Waikoloa Beach Resort), and the Mauna Lani, to name two. Queen's Marketplace has free hula exhibitions every Monday, Wednesday, and Friday evening from 6 to 7 pm. Bring those chairs you bought and get your picnic dinner at the food court nearby. Lot's of fun, and educational.

The Mauna Lani calendar is a little less rigid, but they host a monthly evening of entertainment and storytelling on the Saturday closest to the full moon. Check their calendar for "Twilight at Kalahupua'a."

This event is a bit hard to describe. Danny Akaka Jr., son of former Senator Akaka and a Hawaiian cultural expert, hosts an evening of Hawaiian history and entertainment on the Mauna Lani grounds. It is entertainment you will not find anywhere else, including local music, interviews and stories by locals, etc. If you are interested in Hawaiian culture and are here at the right time, this is a must do. It starts at 5:30 on the Saturday closest to the full moon each month. Get there an hour early, it's so popular with locals that it fills up quickly. It's outdoors, there are chairs but you might plan on bringing mats, towels, or your beach chairs, as well as a picnic dinner. You can pick up good to-go food at the grocery store at the Mauna Lani shopping center.

This is not a widely-advertised activity, although it's been going on for better than 20 years. It is primarily aimed at Mauna Lani guests and local residents, but visitors are always welcome. It's a little hard to get to; basically,

49 Things to do on the Big Island

you go to the normally-off-limits Mauna Lani Beach Club (take the left-most branch at the traffic circle, then keep bearing to the right as you go around the golf course) for parking, then walk by an old Hawaiian fish pond to a historic cottage on the resort grounds. It's a beautiful setting and a memorable experience.

See Manta Rays

The Mauna Kea Resort, north on the Queen Ka'ahumanu Higway almost to Kawaihae, shines a large, bright light on the water at the extreme north end of their beach for several hours each evening, beginning just after twilight. The light attracts plankton, which in turn attracts manta rays to feed on the plankton. You can stand on the rock lookout next to the (of course) Manta and Pavilion Wine Bar, a nice restaurant, and watch the mantas feed for free most nights. The Mauna Kea has valet parking, which will cost a few bucks, or you can walk in from the beach parking. The valet parking is worth the few dollars, since it's pretty dark, and the valet can give you specific directions to the lookout.

Sometimes, for reasons known only to themselves, the 'rays don't come; but all is not lost! The plankton attract fish; big fish, so you still get to see an amazing sight.

Other Fun Things

Take a Hike

The Ala Kahi Trail, or King's Trail, winds for about 175 miles along the coast, from Hawai'i Volcanoes National Park to the northern end of the island. It's not actually a continuous trail; rather, it's a series of segments built by the National Park Service and incorporating earlier Hawaiian trails to allow access to historic and cultural sites. You can pick up segments at any of the resort areas, and at several places along the Kona coast. You can get maps and more information from the National Park Service.

Bird Watching

Many of the "native" birds were brought in by settlers at one time or another, and a lot of them are endangered.

If you want to see Nene, the endangered Hawaiian goose (related to the Canada goose), go to pretty much any golf course, and especially Big Island Country Club. Really. You'll also see mynas, and a host of starlings, finches, and doves everywhere. The saffron finches, so called because of their startling color, are one of my favorites. They have a habit of sitting next to car rear view mirrors admiring themselves, which would be cute except that they are incontinent; you will know when saffron finches have been visiting.

Parrots can be seen sometimes in the upland forest area; there's even a parrot sanctuary along the Mamalahoa Highway south of Kona.

The rainforest around the Thurston Lava Tube in Hawai'i Volcanoes National Park is rich in native species,

49 Things to do on the Big Island

including the rare 'Io, or Hawaiian hawk. Another spot to see forest birds is Kalopa State Recreation Area. More on this spot elsewhere.

Another good spot is the upland forests off of the Saddle Road, near or in Mauna Kea State Park, or a few miles east of the nearby hunter check-in station. You might see Pueo, the Hawaiian owl, there. He can be also be found anyplace the mouse population is booming. Pueo is a serious mouse-hunter who comes out at twilight. They're smaller than barn owls, and no threat to the cat population.

Hakalau National Wildlife Refuge, up country from Hilo, is supposedly the best for the truly serious bird watcher, but you need to make special arrangements well in advance to gain entry. Contact the Refuge Manager in Hilo at 808-933-6915.

There are not a lot of seabird species in Hawai'i. One thing for which we are all grateful is a lack of seagulls. You also won't see hummingbirds; they interfere with the pollination of pineapple.

Other Fun Things

Check out Some Petroglyphs

Before the missionaries came in 1820, there was no such thing as a written Hawaiian language. Hawaiians would sometimes make marks in stone to commemorate events or provide guidance for travelers, or just because they could, although carving lava is a pretty challenging form of graffiti. These stone markings are called petroglyphs, and they're pretty common. You will find them just about everywhere.

49 Things to do on the Big Island

One of the richest petroglyph fields in West Hawai'i is at the Waikoloa Beach Resort on the Kohala Coast, next to the gas station at King's Shops. Park there and just cross the street, follow the very short trail, and you're there. Don't walk on the 'glyphs, they are surprisingly fragile, especially if lots of people walk on them.

Another good one is the Puako Petroglyph Field, near the Fairmont Orchid, in the Mana Lani Resort complex. Turn right at the traffic circle, right again just before the entrance to the hotel, and follow the signs.

The Pu'u Loa Petroglyphs, off of Chain of Craters Road, in Volcanoes National Park, is yet another popular place, marked with signs.

This is by no means all of them; they can be seen on just about any flat surface, it seems like.

Some of them are pretty obvious; turtles look like turtles, stick-figure people look like people, sort-of. The circle-with-a-dot thing is believed to be a place where a newborne infant's umbilical was placed as a connection to the earth. You'll see a lot of those.

You will sometimes see petroglyphs that look like letters; they probably are. Hawaiians took to reading and writing pretty quickly; in fact, by about the mid-19th century, Hawai'i had a 100% literacy rate, and nearly everybody could read and write. Some petroglyphs are carved words, often names or biblical references.

Photographing them is tricky; you want deep shadowing, no flash, and close up.

Other Fun Things

Have Breakfast at a Farmers' Market

Hawai'i Island is agricultural, and quite a bit of food is sold locally at farmers' markets. Seemingly every town worthy of a stop sign has a market.

There's a large, semi-permanent market featuring souvenirs and handcrafts as well as food in Kailua-Kona, right on Ali'i Drive; and another in Hilo, on Kamehameha Avenue. Both run every day except Monday. The smaller towns have markets on Saturday and Wednesday.

Waimea has four separate farmers' markets on Saturday, all of which include stalls selling food to eat right then and there. You can find waffles, barbeque, sandwiches, local specialties, and pretty much anything else that can be prepared on a gas burner. At one market there's even a wood-fired oven baking bread right on the spot.

The farmers' markets get going about sunrise, and are in full swing by 8 am, and sell out by noon, so get there early.

49 Things to do on the Big Island

Afterword

I hope this book, and your trip, has been helpful for you; and more importantly, that you've had fun!

I welcome comments and suggestions -

SaminHawaii@hotmail.com

- and even more, I welcome reviews on Amazon. Reviews are how Amazon rates books. The more reviews there are, the more Amazon believes that it must be a better, or at least more popular, book. So help me out, leave a review.

Mahalo

Sam

Made in the USA
Middletown, DE
10 August 2017